ADVENTIST PIONEER SERIES

# WILLIAM MILLER
## finds a Savior

Written by
**MONIK FOLKMAN**

Illustrated by
**LOLA USUPOVA**

Copyright © 2025 Butter n' Honey
ISBN 978-1-967145-00-3

Illustrated by Lola Usupova
Edited by Rebecca McKinney

Scriptures quoted are from King James Version.
Direct quotes are from *Memoirs of William Miller* by Sylvester Bliss.
Image used is in public domain, author unknown.

More books are coming soon! Go to www.adventistpioneerseries.com.

"Suddenly, the character of a Saviour was vividly impressed upon my mind. It seemed that there might be a Being so good and compassionate as to himself atone for our transgressions, and thereby save us from suffering the penalty of sin. I immediately felt how lovely such a Being must be; and imagined that I could cast myself into the arms of, and trust in the mercy of, such an One. But the question arose, How can it be proved that such a Being does exist? Aside from the Bible, I found that I could get no evidence of the existence of such a Saviour, or even of a future state. I felt that to believe in such a Saviour without evidence would be visionary in the extreme. I saw that the Bible did bring to view just such a Saviour as I needed..."

– William Miller

William Miller was an American farmer known for saying that Jesus was coming very soon. His message caused a great spiritual revival in America in the mid–1800s, and many people surrendered their hearts to Jesus.

However, William had not always been concerned with spiritual matters.

From a very young age, William was a bright boy who learned self-denial, responsibility, and hard work. He was the oldest and grew up on a farm in Low Hampton, New York, with fifteen brothers and sisters.

He learned about patriotism and piety from his parents. His father, Captain William Miller, was a soldier during the American Revolution who later became a farmer. His mother, Paulina, was a prayerful woman who was the daughter of a Baptist minister.

William, however, had much to learn about being religious. In fact, one of the things he liked to do was make fun of his Grandfather Phelps, a devout Baptist minister, and his uncle, Elihu Miller, who was also a pastor. Though he was respectful in their presence, William secretly mocked them in front of his friends by imitating how they talked.

William's behavior greatly saddened his mother. She shared her worry with Grandfather Phelps. He was very wise and said, "Don't afflict yourself too deeply about William. There is something for him to do yet in the cause of God!"

Deep down, William longed for God's acceptance. He thought about it and planned, "I will do nothing wrong, tell no lies, and obey my parents." But he soon found his promises to be weak and soon broken.

So he thought, "I will give up the things I love the most."
Again, this did not bring joy to his heart.

When he was older and married, he befriended men who were kind and had good morals. But these men rejected the Bible and believed in a God who created the world and left it to run on its own. His friends were called deists. Unfortunately, William left the Baptist faith of his mother and adopted their beliefs.

Though William found the Bible difficult to understand at times,
he did not feel it safe or wise to abandon it completely like
other deists until he found something more trustworthy.
This was his safety.

Then came the Battle of Plattsburgh, a turning point in the War of 1812—and William's spiritual life. It happened on September 11, 1814, while William served as a captain in the American army. The British were ready to attack with 15,000 men and a well-equipped fleet of ships on Lake Champlain. William and his men had little faith in their small army. With just 1,500 soldiers and 4,000 volunteers, defeat seemed inevitable.

William fought bravely, but there was heavy fire all around him. When three of the men nearest to him were injured, William realized it was a miracle that he was unharmed. Even more miraculous was the American's victory! The battle was so unbelievable that William became convinced it was the work of a Mightier Power.

After his military life, William eventually moved back to Low Hampton near his family farm. There he attended the little church his uncle pastored. When his uncle could not come, a deacon would read a sermon. William felt that the way the deacons read was uninspiring. He volunteered to read even though he still struggled with his belief in God.

Two years passed, bringing about another turning point in William's life. It happened while William and his helpers were planning a celebration for the anniversary of the Battle of Plattsburgh. While preparing, William and his helpers were curious about a religious service being held the night before the grand event and decided to attend.

The preaching, which was based on Zechariah 2:4, left a great impression on William and his helpers. William never forgot the words, "Run! Speak to this young man!" He was so touched that he could not continue with the preparations for the battle celebration. Instead of festivity, his heart was filled with prayer and praise.

The following day was William's turn to read a sermon. But as he read, he felt such strong emotions about his sin that he could not continue. The picture of a wonderful Savior was clearly imprinted on his mind—a Being so good and kind that forgives and saves from sin. William marveled at how lovely it could be to trust in such a Being. Oh, how he longed to be accepted.

But how could he find Him?

Years before, William had almost rejected the Bible. But it was in the Bible that William found Jesus! Studying the Bible not only led him to accept Jesus as his Savior, but it became a delight, and he discovered a message that sparked a great spiritual revival in America.

Some people travel far and wide in search of truth. Some go through many life experiences, while others read books to find a Savior. Yet all along, as William discovered, the Bible is the surest place to find Jesus.

*"Search the scriptures... they are they which testify of me."*
John 5:39

# WILLIAM MILLER

### February 15, 1782
William Miller was born in Pittsfield, Massachusetts.

### 1786
William Miller and his family moved to Low Hampton, New York. This was the place where William grew up. He was homeschooled by his mother until the age of nine and then attended East Poultney School District.

He did not receive formal schooling after the age of 18.

### June 29, 1803
William Miller married Lucy Smith. Afterwards, the newlyweds moved to Poultney, Vermont. They had ten children, eight of which lived to adulthood.

### July 21, 1810
William Miller was commissioned as a lieutenant in the army.

### February 1, 1814
William Miller was promoted to captain by the President of the United States.

### September 11, 1814
The Battle of Plattsburgh commenced. This battle was part of the War of 1812, and it was the battle that ended the British invasion of the northern states of the United States. This battle was one of the turning points in William Miller's conversion.

### June 18, 1815
William Miller was discharged from the army and returned to Poultney.

### September 1816
William Miller was converted after listening to a sermon by a doctor who preached before the celebration of the anniversary of the Battle of Plattsburgh, and on the next day, while reading a sermon at church, he received a vivid impression of the Savior. He soon started studying the Bible.

## 1818

William made a solemn conclusion from his study of the 2300-day prophecy that Jesus was to come again sometime between March 21st, 1843, and March 21st, 1844, according to the Jewish calendar. He was reluctant to share his study and kept studying to make sure he had the right interpretation.

## 1823

William Miller started to feel the burden to share with others, but still feeling hesitant, he only shared with friends and acquaintances.

## August 1833

William made a promise to God that he would preach about Jesus's coming upon invitation only. To his surprise, he received an invitation half an hour later. The next day, he preached his first sermon on the topic in a town called Dresden.

## Spring 1843

Jesus did not come as William Miller predicted. William Miller and others who followed his message, called the Millerites, were disappointed.

## August 1844

Samuel Snow presented that the 2300-day prophecy ended on October 22, 1844, which he thought would be the day when Jesus would come.

## October 22, 1844

Jesus did not come, and there was a great disappointment among the Millerites.

## December 20, 1849

William Miller died in full faith that Jesus would return soon.

February 15, 1782 - December 20, 1849

www.ingramcontent.com/pod-product-compliance
Lightning Source LLC
Chambersburg PA
CBHW041445120626
46547CB00002B/357